BURNING THROUGH

BURNING THROUGH

Elizabeth McKim

Visual Interpretation by

Jose L. Delgado Guitart

Grateful Acknowledgement is made to the
following magazines in which some of these
poems first appeared: *Grist, Ploughshares,
Pyramid, The Stone, The Little Magazine,
Poetry, Epoch, Sidelines, Moving Out, Sun-
bury, Blackberry, Pendulum, Dark Horse,
The Blacksmith Anthology, River Styx,
13th Moon,* and *Tendril.*

Composition and design by George E. Murphy Jr.
Front and back cover graphics by Jose L. Delgado-Guitart

Library of Congress Catalog Number: 78-54035
ISBN 0-931694-01-9

First Edition
May 1978

for my daughter Jenny

≪ CONTENTS ≫

Visual Interpretations by Jose L. Delgado-Guitart
Covers and pps. 13, 27, 53, 81, 89.

How The Women's Revolution Came
To Pass

I met Elizabeth McKim in the early 1970's when we were both attending workshops at Ottone Riccio's Hellric House in Jamaica Plain, Massachusetts. She arrived one morning wearing a black leotard and a long flower print skirt. It was April and she was beautiful and thin with the direct eyes of a person intent on knowing you.

For the most part, until she came along, we were a group of housewife poetasters at Riccio's afraid to take the risk of committing ourselves entirely to a life's work that had sent so many of our role models into alcoholic rehabilitation programs, bedlam, or the arms of Old Man Suicide. Our poems were full of the kinds of images that Freud would have gotten an erection over and that Jill Johnston would have thrown up over. We wrote about "creaming pitchers", "fathers who entered us", and "long, hot, syringes filling us with love".

We struggled so to validate the very real oppression we felt as daughters, mothers, wives, and citizens that we often unconsciously lifted entire stanzas from Plath and Sexton and juxtaposed them between our whining own. But then Elizabeth McKim arrived carrying the first manuscript in progress that I had ever seen and frankly it changed me from a woman with an axe to grind into a poet with a conscience. The poems she brought to class that day make up this book.

Slowly, carefully, and with professional detachment Elizabeth began to read. Immediately a rush of adrenalin stung me fully awake to her historic 10 a.m. delivery. In a rich and powerful voice Elizabeth created image by image an exciting new archetype: The Liberated Woman. Not the woman we, as victims, were supposed to grow into becoming. Not the woman that MS magazine said was already here, sharing the housework and childcare with androgynous spirits, who by virtue of their genitals were classified as men. No, Elizabeth's Liberated Woman was as ordinary as a sock. She did what she did because she was born free and the world, all of it, from Boston to Bombay belonged to her.

the smell of our bodies after we have tasted   the smell
of hands and hair of belly and flank the sex smell
of eyes when you look at me after

And this is how it came to pass that I realized the second wave of women's struggle towards liberation had already hit the shore. The wheels of revolution had spun full circle and stopped as Elizabeth McKim's voice articulated the first authentically guiltless female being. It will be a century before the rest of us catch up to her. Meanwhile we can look forward to more of her flip, magical, and experimental work. She is the cosmic consciousness broken through the decadence of dottering, patristic reflection. She is the beginning

and the before
and the now at last...

Terry Kennedy
Anno Feminarum 1978

9

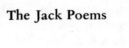

The Jack Poems

The Heavy Object

Many times
I heard the voice
of the heavy object.
Behind closed doors.
Through small holes.
Across frontiers at dawn.
Many times I was too pressed
down to meet the object.
Much less to move it.
At those times I stopped.
Wanting a cool forest.
Its resting places.
My legs were so tired
they could not carry me
and I slept.
I balanced
small perfect circles
on the outside edge of my dreams.
I danced with the heavy object
which turned and turned
until it was green and manageable,
until we held each other and wept,
until I could speak directly
to the heavy object,
until I could work with it slowly,
until we could restore each other,
until I could regain what I knew as a child:
a real bird, a mountain, a snail all coral
in the shape of a realizable mountain,
a circle above another circle
below, three roads leading
to the sky, and the sky
completely emptied
of any object
completely
free.

Ladies And Gentlemen

It is time to say
what I have come to say.

I take out my little woven bag
and there is nothing.
It's nothing I say
trying to convince you
that this is what I came for
this is what I always wanted.

I take out my shoes.
They no longer have oarlocks
or oars, to take me across
or through.

I take out my hat.
It no longer has horns,
or fur.

I take out my hands.
They no longer have claws.

I take out my arms.
They no longer have wings.

And my eyes.
The miraculous secrets
have drifted off
quite quietly.

As for my sex
it has lost its metaphors.
Magnolia blossoms
mix with the earth
and disappear.
Leaving only a strong smell.
Strong I say.

And now to the nose.
It no longer follows strangers
who beckon at night from bridges.
Who wave saxophones.
Who own prowed boats.
Who talk in the fog.

And look at the breasts.
They are no longer watchers.
Or little friends. Or fisher-
people. Look at them.
They look back.

And the belly
is no longer showing off.
No longer the wise grandma.
The grumbler. The lion-
tamer. The musical instrument.

As for me
I walk through town alone.
Astounded, crying for the first time
in years, counting telephone poles,
reciting names, suddenly
I remember what I came to say to you.

Opening

You loved its color. It was exotic and kind and
homespun and mysterious, and when it laughed, it
gathered you up in wild wheat, and you could talk
to it and respect its mind, and tell it about your
mother who possessed you and your father who dis-
possessed you, and you knew you wanted to feel it,
and if it touched you, you would touch it back,
you kept thinking about it, you had known something similar, it was older but you felt it was
the right moment for something older, so you came
to it in December in the rain, you rang its bell
and when it opened the door you knew how you looked,
and there were drops of rain on your thin blond
hair and in the panes of your glasses, and you smiled
and said can I come in, and you stayed and cooked
dinner for her, and you told stories to each other
through that first long night, and she wore a brown
velvet dress with a lining the color of peaches
and you knew you would be back. You loved her now
the mother and now the child, and you closed your
eyes and whispered yes and then went back across
the MTA tracks and got your belongings your statue
of Shiva your batik from Benares, and your books on
Trollope and Conrad, and when you came back you
brought strawberries and grapes and a talisman
from Japan, and you made up a story to make it magic
and it wasn't until later you told her you had
made it up.

There Is A Man

inside me.
As terrible as myself.

Sometimes at night
he scratches at my funny bone
and rubs. Whispers
hot music.

There is a man.
I used to watch him waving
in the tall field grass
behind my house.
He followed me to the city.
I found him raking litter
in an unspecified spot.

He beckoned me back to his place
and laid me on a wood-sleek table.
With the lick of a cat
he pounced and poured me down
like an oyster.

My eyes grew round and blissful.
There is a man inside me
as terrible as myself.

Jack Of The Heart

of the scar
of the ripped sleep
freezing me out
where I can't grab on
can't tramp through
anything but silver
little brother   wolf
man of my hands
and knees
I'm down
I'm scrubbing past
I'm making my own heat
collecting splinters
trying to let go
what we once held
huddled up against
the spine of our pain
do something
act quickly
tell the old stories
war atrocities
road shows
last minute deals
pushovers
sugar
sugar
the ice mounts
goes for the heart
like a divining stick
detects our traces
finally our blood
something definite
and red

Note:

I want
to give it
to ya

shoot it
up
your spine

shootit
tup
shoo shoo
tit
tituu
ap yap
your tap
ahh
your sss
aaagh
s pin
pine
spine
a famous line

Sniper

I'm impressed.
Slowly I take off your clothes
and taste your exaggeration.

You lift me off the sand-floor
and spin me   shoot it
up my spine.

I'm impressed.
Then I realize it's another woman.
It's her spine you want

to shoot it into.
I'm crushed.
But then you say you love me

say its like constructing
a beautiful box
slowly   and with much care

nothing slip-
shod   the best materials you say
you want to learn your craft

unfold this lotus
this sun has caught you now.
You are all the sea.

Your eyes are glinting.
Near us harbor seals dip.
We play like porpoises.

Suddenly
you push me into dunes.
Aim whole handfuls of grit

into my open place.
The air swarms with smithereens.
Between blasts someone is groaning.

Bending near me you ask
if there is sand in *your* eyes.
I'm not sure what you mean anymore.

You say your real name is Jack.
You fire a boulder over your shoulder
for luck. It rolls down dunes turning to salt.

Then into tears which the gulls carry away.
The sea turns to meat.
The sea turns to metal.

You say 'never trust the Sandman.'
You ask if we can still be friends.
You walk away.

My Message

do you intend
to give it back
or what

filled with holes
stuffed with poems
there is nothing
do you feel it

insisting this is not
a poem
nothing changes
turns blue

as winter
i am parted
in the middle
i have no-

where to go
i have to get there soon
i can't hold onto
these lights   this scaffolding

these rafters   this is not
a poem   you are
the roof on my house
has blown off

the wind has turned
it into something
which can't be
written   my head

is a tough pumpkin
but once the skin is broken
into   it's all over
the broken fool:

a whole puzzle
contains my pieces
decides not to give
them back -- at the far table

the other people talk
a strange language
we dispossess
the wind changes

something sinister
enters the room   the people
tell us to get lost
we are al-
ready there

it is time
i found my way
through the window
the wind has entered
you singing
dancing

    Jack, i...
let it go
this is no poem

You Bastard Jack

Flat on my back   Jack
and singing
asking   even pleading
for the old one two
buckle my shoe
Jack   I'm not too old
I can still sing
Jack my knife
My jolly jump up
Stick in your thumb
Carry me to market
Be quick
Be candle
O Goddammit   Jack
Be wise

Fable Of The Broken Fool

One night, lying awake, I noticed the lids shaking,
also unlocked, also unhealed. I approached sound-
lessly, gently pried them open to allow a slit of
light. In that first instant, the whole carnival
came pressing out, as if from two underground tunnels.
There were wild beasts, glittering girls in black
masks, freaks, jugglers, high-wire dancers, flame
swallowers, the fat man, and in the middle was the
broken fool, coming apart and smiling. I had nowhere
to go. I moved toward him, begging him with my eyes
to let me put him together again. And when the last
piece was found and firmly secured, he leaned toward
me to kiss my eyes in gratitude, and before I knew
what was happening, he had sucked them out as if
they were hard candy. His mouth full, he was still
able to hum as he began to break again. As for me,
I have been in darkness ever since. I still have my
lids, but they close over empty rooms. At night I
dream about the circus and the broken fool, his smile,
his breaking sound.

Love Is After The Storm

1.
love is after
the storm slouched
in a heap in the corner

love sees through
clouded eyes
sees a rainbow

now the storm
has no place to hide
love hangs on anyway

says look storm   no hands
and storm expands
says babe let's split

says this is it
love cleans drawers
waits   leaves notes   smokes

packs   but the storm
doesn't call back
how 'bout that

2.
so love shuts down
her lids hunch over her
dreams the mountain lies

between the crows which circle the peak
and the mildewed cows which look
at night to the top and moo

and love is swollen and grey
when the storm comes back
goes down on her covers her dark

3.
like a rainbow
storm sings   soaping
himself all over
with love's commercials

croons as she sudses
and rubs him up
with her orange works
her blue into

a froth spreads
mm mmm green lather
into a million dancing
bubbles like a rainbow

love shouts
obscene instructions
bits of erotica
from the love manual
as she zooms
down the drain
in a whoshshshs
and the storm
predictable
as menstruation
leans into the next
adventure
flies south
for the sun

Prediction

you will
go home
it will
be cold
you will
warm some-
one
your sister
your cousin
a girl
you meet
in a park
in a bar
her elbows
red
with waiting
you will
clap your mittens
on
her ears
you will sing
songs
from the frozen territory
you will stir
her slowly
and the wind will blow
off the lake your mother
will greet the masseuse
and you will not come down
for days and your father
will ask
about your future
my runaway sun   my

floater   my
ruined plan
and i
shall send you
hollyhock
seeds for the spring
we want
to bloom
and you will
remember
it will
come to you as a cutting
pain in the
gut
it will
grow like a star
when night
comes on
one time
in love
one time
in the after-
noon   you found
my socks
didn't match
didn't match
at all
and at that
disconnected fact
you will
cry out
as wounded things
cry out

Jack Gets It On With Mother Goose

Jack wants it
her garden grows
the goose wanders
it follows her to school
Jack wants it
the cock crows
the spider sits
she is frightened
he sticks his thumb in
they lick the platter clean
upstairs and downstairs they wander
she is frightened
they have a great fall
Jack wants it
she jumps over the candlestick
he sticks his thumb in
she licks the platter clean
he is nimble
she will eat no lean
the spider sits
she is frightened
he jumps over
she blows his horn
her garden grows
the dish runs away
he sticks his thumb in
the goose wanders
they lick the platter clean
it was against the rules
they lick the platter clean

Jack:

When you said you wanted   out
I readied for war.
My teeth grew razor sharp.
My howl was aimed to kill
your roots and roses.
My family said they'd help.

Jack:
when you left
I fingered my lonely holes
and bled for months.
Maybe years.
It's women's work.
Jack:
I'm tired of the work!
And more important.
There are other struggles.

The window grows each day.
The door swings out.
The gate keeps nothing in.
Down the streets
there are people
just like you and me.

Jack:
The world is breaking up.
Coming back together
I see it differently.

Attack

I am the woman
who rides the freights

you can see me any night
my chin in the wind

one hand holding the rails
the other holding on
my own body
I pretend is still there
when you say you have to say

goodby
I hold
your goodby
in my stomach
I lay my belly
on the flat whistle
of your goodby

the old language will not do for this
the charred gutterals of tramps
barrels of sperm oil   cargo of mother tongue
I cross the wheatfields into kansas
a blur of farmers stand in rows

I spot the slave master
he is smiling   clicking his fingers
suddenly spits through his teeth
i try to focus on the friends
the women   the children

even the backs of my legs
are charged with this
tension   the eye
listens for the far corner
of my sex   I gather
momentum
stroke the wheel
my stomach
into a rage
of sharp activity

you proceed me
down miles of track
I holler before
my heart strikes

between rails
in sunlit clover
I lay you out
sweet and still
as a sleeping child

The Opening And Closing

of petals sleek as the backs of fish
their gills opening into the black
spreading out into a darker ink
closing out the wide field of day
the sureness   the depth of the woman
the man in the mirror behind her   the darkness
behind him   the way their eyes open   the way
the world closes   the laundry outside
filling with wind   creasing back
into a pocket   the morning sun
stretches into afternoon   marking sun-
down the whole stain of day   the birds heel out
into the wound   the dark closes in
as I open to my love as he closes we become
the secret petals pulse the house
the prisoner the presence the furthest exit
now he opens as I close I remember scenes
I didn't expect the young Vietnamese whose mouth
opens onto mine and burns mine closed my eyes leap
into my daughters open face in fright in friendliness
my mother's shoulders clap her closed and rounded off
as I close over the final fact   now open
and staring a fish closed and hooked
slapping its bloody weight
across the open deck

Poem For A New Home

I.
I guess at these dwelling places
the old charred camping grounds
somebody's hand-me-down chateau
a cave in the south
where people with real eyes
stare out of hollows
whisper hello

so long jack

II.
o these stabilized houses with double locks
have pursued me panting overweight
down front walks clipped hedges bicycles
with training wheels

o my heart is a sensuous house
where i arch my back on velvet pillows

so long jack

III
You find me
barely breathing
in a huge stern edifice

even the pigeons
find the place
unlivable

the story goes
how I burst open the sky-
light and the whole

construction collapses
like a pod in late summer.
People run out

from under
a real blow-
up

I under-
stand

so long
so long jack
i have to go

IV.
I lived for a while
under a boulder
a heavy sea-
pocked thing
a father rock

How I suffered
enduring such sea-
punctures
belches

passive
I rubbed dumbly
against whales
walruses

everything ponderous
till one day I broke
in a burst of sun
and said simply

38

enough
enough commotion
enough of this heavy scene

V.
Touched
I lived in a forest
where animals twanged

and yelped
I played Snow White
asked gently

is somebody home
no one was
I was

shouting now
caught up
in the crazy

dark
and no
place to go

VI.
believe me
I was glad
you came
when you did

when you left
I slept on your name

so long Jack
so long since then
and everywhere I am
is where I live
is home
is where I am

Listen Jack The Answer Is

You sniff me out.
Decide I'm the one.
A certain vulnerable look
about the eyes. A strength
in the hips. For you   an older woman.
The smell of your mother.
The spell of your aunt when you were nine.
The woman you loved and buried.
The woman who buried you
and went to Vermont wearing purple.
You come over unasked wearing purple.
You wake me up from naps to ask if I'm wearing
purple. You call after midnight.
You tell me I'm cosmic.
You wonder if I'm orgasmic.
You wonder if since there's a full moon
I'd like to drive to Worcester for ice cream.
You want to get stoned with me, take acid trips.
You wonder if I want to go to bed.
You wonder if me and my daughter would like to move in.
You wonder if I can ever leave you.
You wonder if you can put the tooth fairy under your pillow.
You wonder if gently, so very gently I'd hardly feel it
you can press into me harder and harder
hardly leaving a trace after you've entered
Listen Jack the answer is

I want to say it
          clearly
I want to speak it out slowly shape it in my mouth
          break my fast with it
Feel the texture and color of it each time
I wear it simply and with ease
          I want to send it flying in my fist
In my voice In the strength of my dance
          I want to roll with it down hills
I want to sleep with it join my family with it
I want to say it listen Jack

the answer's no

Season Of The Old Crone

She Comes To Me In A Dream

She arrives on the oldest night of the year.
 Under her tongue is lava not yet hard.
 She is dressed in gold. Behind her
  is a country at night. At war.
   And behind that, fireworks, ironworks,
    a million stars. She takes my hand
     and looks me down the years to my beginning.
      She asks me questions which fall like petals,
       which sequester in groups, which recreate
        old situations, which rise
         like banners in the smoke.

She tells me she knows where I was born.
 She tells me she knows I didn't mean
  to let the baby hit the ground.
   She tells me she knows I hide
    strange vines and languages
     beneath the words I do not dare to breathe.
She tells me I have yet to be born into my skin,
 into the real nature of my crimes, into my first No,
  into my ruins. She tells me it will come and I will rise.
   She tells me to be easy. She says I have to wait.

She asks me what has become of the dark-eyed man.
 I tell her he lives somewhere else. I tell her we meet
  occasionally under the bridge of Avignon
   the one that goes half way across. I tell her
    I call to him when I drive alone in my car.
     She smiles. She knows of this desire.
      She tells me to take off my clothes.
       She says I will not catch fire.
        I will not turn into my mother.
         I will not start to snow.

She tells me not to be afraid.
 She tells me she does not know how to waltz.
  She tells me to keep turning.
   She tells me news of the fat girl
    the one who died in childbirth
     the one with the sweat stains
      down to her waist
       the one who tried to poison me
        deliberately. She tells me I am not kind.
       She tells me it is not important.
        She tells me I will get along without her.
        She tells me what I always knew.
         She leaves me how I always am.

Season Of The Old Crone Blossoming

The old crone pads through orchards of her ordering,
tossing garlands, spitting seeds and wishing on them,
flinging apple cores sky-high she rolls tears
down her cheeks like birthdays in the center of her age.

The sun laps her up. Children play in her rafters
shouting *leap-frog, leap-frog*. At noon no one finds her
home. She swims in the wind in a clear pond where gold-
fish run the waters. On shore she shakes whole schools

of drops from her back, whistles, dances inside
circles inside circles, and lets go, and lets go.

Exit

Roses.
Crushed petals
everywhere.

Even stuck on the walls.
She is scolded again
about this messiness.

The radio reminds her
to hang on.
The paper slings

suicide.
The subway
relocates the tunnel.

Once again Sunday.
Baked bread and the Boston

Globe Sunday.
The door slides shut.
The old crone mutters

pretty kitty
pretty kitty

2.
Outside in the meadow
orange birds leap
from the lime-green field.

There is someone
shuffling at the doorstep.
She can't see him.
She can tell she loves him.

3.
Bees gather.
Bridges burn halfway across.
The children have arrived.

Their faces flushed
they come arm in arm
singing all the old songs.

Sur le pont
d'Avignon

They move between prisms.
Sliced sections of light.
Film strip. Xerox.

Heavy steps clump
into a fat face.
Melt like butter

into a high voice saying
The children are armed!
The alarm reactivates
down the concrete steps.

4.
It's time
she makes her getaway
through the children
who have shot up
like bayonets.

They are all there.
They are all in drag.
They are wearing masks
and their father's smiles.

No one talks.
She thinks
someone is in trouble.

On her way to the sea
there is a black car.
Silver accessories
shine in the flat sun.

Behind the car
a golden sheet
of desert.

Beyond that
the sea.

5.
She has always wanted.
Always been wanting.

Her keys
have all left.
But one.

Catches the light.
Blisters her palm.

No living creature sighs.
As she slides off.

I'd Slide Out Of My Life

sun on the door
spilling on the side
walk to town   hop
a quiet trolley
to the greyhound

terminal   sleep all the way
to iowa   find a small
town with one main street
one all night diner
get a job

feeding truckers   slapping
down sunny-side-ups   buttering
englishes   pocketing
dimes   hum with the juke
till three   make it

home alone
sun in a while
coming up hungry red and mean

I would lean into life
like a pilot or a dancer

I would change my name
Sundays I would bowl

Winter Solstice

Filled with forgiveness for what she wants,
all she gets is the ancient hole.
Its dark. Its repetitious. Its shores.

The runes on the hill are winter-killed.
The stars cluck like chickens in a barnyard.
She makes love to herself, croons herself

back to sleep, drops like a green stone
through long passageways of green. Looking
down, she is appalled by the constancy

of seedlings. Looking off, she swallows
her old age and swims toward the infant
she knows she is, her face obscured by vines.

Woman With Milkweed Meets Man From Deep Inside Whale

we are stolen from ourselves
and lent to others whom we do not know

We graze in shining pastures
  and in the dark we darkly move.
He shows me heart-pink coral reefs,
  golden sun-fish laying out in water-stripes.
He tells me of the killer and his teeth,
  of babies, how they sleep beneath
their mother's fins, of the long migrations,
  and after, in the summer shoals,
how they rock and play for hours,
  slapping the waves with their great flukes

whale willow whale big fish
willow why will you now
whistle low how I wish
whale willow whaling fish

I talk of raspberries and burrs,
  canteloupe, and how the maple leaves go fiery
in the fall. I show him jagged glass from the dry
  land, and trash, the ghostliness of dumps,
how vultures tear at meat, how cars in thousands
  drowse in fields once turned and farmed.

my wish is a wind-wish
my wound is a weathered wound
my song is a silver fish
my tear is a sea-tune

We lie together in a huge space
  and feed on milkweed,
found high in meadows after summer,
  small fluff-seeds in a bark canoe,
packed and ready to take off.
  Milkweed! Catapulting out the spout-
hole like rice at a wedding, quilting the sea
  with field dreaming, tossed higher and higher,
spiralling up into the mean wind
  and gnaw of gulls, like lazy curlicues
of smoke. We turn, we turn the sea, we turn
  it into more than what it is,
and what it is is more than we can know.

Deluge

The telephone splutters,
throws up other swimmers,
unlisted drownings.

The operator is hysterical,
says she never learned
to swim. The table's lost
its fat legs. The chair
doubles over and splats
on the floor.

The ceiling groans,
says it can cave in
at any time, but

> *the water is silver*
> *and could be*
> *i am past drowning*
>
> *i rely on*
> *the breast-stroke*
> *to keep me alive*

I focus on a country house:
white shingles, surrounded
by birch trees, catbirds,

and medium sized rocks. I pull
myself in the lower story
window, and climb the front

stairs toward the bedroom.
There is a dark-
haired child in my old bed.

Nothing in her moves
when she says she will not
come out to drown.

Menace

You come where snowy egrets meet,
where curlews nest;
You come where rare, ungainly birds,
desert-bred, find
for the first time, wide water ways.

You come where thick-beaked parent birds
nestle into eaves.
Far into the night they talk; later they mourn
the cousins in a jar;
 It could happen to you
 It could happen to you...

Still as a signpost on the edge
of the Tuscawilla Prarie, you wait;
I feel the sweat of your endurance, the coil
of your hunger, the hard agate of your pupils,
the low coo you have learned to simulate. Sure

as slang in the grass, all dew and motion,
you come where snowy egrets meet, where curlews nest.

Mud Pudding

Mud Pudding, the birds scream.
He fluctuates, tries to call them
off, recalls the soft hide of his mother.
Mud Pudding! Mockingbirds hook cruel

remarks on the air while he sloshes
in heavy skin among the open streams
of water lilies. The sky is a blanket
of birds now, they dive into his ears,

leave barbs in his dreams, beads
on his back. He sighs for a mate, one
he might have been in another life,
garlanded by musk and blossom, heavy-

limbed, and finally hot, wanting only
him. *Mud Pudding* the birds shout.
He crashes into vines, trailing
sodden tangles of earth, wet veins.

A scratch from his flank draws the slow laugh
of blood. He heaves a monumental bank of flesh
down on dirt, surrounded by vacant air, elastic,
going on forever. Beside him, male and female

sleep, their breath synonomous.
Mud Pudding whimpers, cries for green
expanding where someone waits, still a pin-

point, an egg teetering on the horizon
till she bends, beckons, spills out in a rush.

Break In Waltz Time

the daydone is falling
the roomer is peeking
he begs for an armful
the woman feels peaked
the menses are coming
the lovers are waltzing
the piglets are suckling
the mamas are crooning
the daydone is swelling
the roomer is swaying
is pecking the pillow
is crying the soldiers
are bleeding are calling
for shelter the iceman
is smiling the window
is breaking the woman
is falling the lovers
are faking are crying
the piglets are whining
the woman is bleeding
is hungry the soldiers
are waltzing the sunrise
is bleeding the daybreak
is cracking the woman
is melting the window
the woman is breaking

The wall, the terror of the wall, the horror of
the brick, the deep snow on the face of the wall,
the child on the face of the stone, and still, and
all alone, and the deep well of the child, and all
alone, and the snow on the stone, and one stone of
snow, and simply running away, and not being able to
sleep after that, and running down the street, and
running, and running through nights after that, not
fit to run, feet falling behind me, and snow coming
down, and the snow coming harder, and the snow, and
my friend's face after that turning to snow, and the
snow beginning, all night the snow coming, the soft
feel of the snow, softly all night falling and looking
up seeing snow like stones and hearing the window sing
and the wind coming up and knowing what I lose what
I have lost the stones moving into the snow and never
mind the snow coming harder finally forming a face at
the window cold as snow the child calling out afraid
if there is finally no noise she will turn into snow
never melting will turn the snow finally knowing no
way out, no way out no way out and the stone the one
stone calling out...

Alcoholic

the dark shadow-bottle
the mother-mouth
the first door
the last exit
the fire-lane
the birth
the law

oh this woman holds her bottle
oh this baby holds her mother
it's a secret she can't bear to hear it
throws her out now in the snowbank
mama what the hell you doing
in a snowbank naked
when the neighbors might be looking
for the whiskey in the whiteness
mama didn't mean to do it mama

hunched over she catches
herself retrieves the bottle
lapses into dreams she is a seal
noses orange balls when she wakes she slips
into gold color of lightning
shuffles and struts to her circus trainer
life boom boom life this perfect
life this life

Here The Cry Is The Only Thing

Nothing budges the small mouth,
the child's plea flattened under the ice,
asking to go home. Words mark the air
like long lashes of northwind biting her back.

Nothing honks here, and this is real,
this is a well. She touches silver
walls, the surface now a skating rink
where children glide in circles, shining
of winter and the gosling's grey coat.

When can I go home, the voice repeats.
And here is the sandman. He's come to bargain.
Passive and sullen, she tells him she knows
what he's come for. He tells her to take off
her clothes. *It's winter,* she says, *and besides,*

this well is a skating pond. They place a heap
of sandstone on the ice between them and begin
to chip away at it. They don't know what will survive:
pact or offering, some ritual from the past.
On the surface of the well, the ice is smooth
as the initiation of a dream. Here, children glide

in glistening black arcs, pipers from another world.
They cry, *you can't get home, you can't get through the ice!*
Suddenly, the ice splits open, cuts the sky into splinters,
into sparks, as something turns and balances below.

Burning Through

Her face melts. Her mouth opens. I hear her. I run
through all her rooms. All her doors are open. The curtains
are burning. She sits into herself. She is calling. I
run to her. She is my doll. I hold her in my arms. I
rock her. I tell her the old stories. We repeat the old
crimes. I hum to her. She is quiet now. I let her drop.

    and something drops out of my body and rolls under
    the bed and I wake up I put my hands in my lap
    I fold into myself I hum I sit in a tree I watch
    the house I wait

It will happen by itself. It will begin. I will sit in
my tree and watch. I will nod and watch. I will hum
and watch. The curtains blowing will burn slowly in and out.

It

was on the roof they say
  the edge of the roof
    it was close to the sky they say
      they knew it had felt rain
        it went away they say
          they never heard from it again they say
            they never knew the words it might have shaped
            they never saw it moving through

flame, the passge of seasons, birth, the mating cries,
  they never cared, they never wanted it, or
    its issue, its mother, its friends,
      they had other things to do,

          they were getting on in the world
            with lives of their own,
              they weren't interested,
              that is definite, they
              couldn't care, they
              hadn't the time,
                so they stopped
                  thinking about it
                    after it went away

But sometimes at night ,when they
   lie together, and the air is
      still, and they have nowhere to go,
         and thoughts blow in and out
            like lights in the sky,
               they wonder; they look
                  around, they hear a
                     rustling in the
                        room, they hear
                           a rustling;
                              they know
                                 they don't want to
                                    know, but
                                       they know

they don't say anything to each
   other, but they know,
      and their eyes close like locked doors,
         and their fingers grasp
            each other, and their
               breath holds
                  them tight and scared
                     and when they dream

   they see it And they see it And they see it AND THEY SEE

Elastic String Dance For Two Voices In Lent

I talk

    of leaves their veins and underbellies
    their ices and their sweat-drops
    i talk of river flow stuck logs

    washed over and over going nowhere
    i talk of stones their wordless pilgrimages
    their beards their clarity i talk

    of freight trains hung around
    perpetual bends and for an instant
    the child's frightened eyes

    at the window asking
    not ever in the world
    to be lost

You talk

    of blood persistent as the Ganges
    of teeth which hollow out whole coconuts
    of toes which clutch on jungle vines and cling

    you talk of the mouth as pleas as heart
    the cunt's uncontrollable tic the pestering cock
    the stomach as controlling stone

spatulate fingers
opening a dwelling place
a child's hiding house
where birth place meets mating moon you talk

We speak

finally of our deaths

I look

at you and break into bells I say
the bells are moving out all over town

You ask

how

Issue

this woman dances wrings hands
does hand-stands washes rings
dusts drifts over snow wonders
what to do what to do next

concentrates on scents and accents
of groceries leaves dreaming
her hands hung down she stands
in streams of soap flakes among

the bit-ends she rocks cold
thoughts heave underground
her breasts like fists shake
alive she crudely bursts shoves

off her skin her precious skin
throws out her rage into the wind
her self her new mad rustling self

Coup

Overnight her mother crawls into her,
fills her with grocery lists,
ammunitions, cleansing
powders, a recipe for brisket.

Overnight her mother takes her poem
and packs it, so tight it cannot breathe,
presses it into four young folds,
puts it in a dark place

with the love letter, the marble,
the chart of the moon, the man
in the moon, the map of the Paris Metro.

And on the night of her mother's takeover,
she hears the brush of tan animals
close to the river; in the thicket

she senses them, even in the darkness
she smells their panic, she knows
their passage. She sees the comet

dive into black waves, she witnesses
a total eclipse of kites, and in the furthest
corner of the nursery she screams, a crumpling

thing stumbles and falls in the stunning blows,
a young torn animal moves through fields of light.

She Chants In The Dark To Keep The Desert Back

in a hot town
in a strange land
but not afraid

on a sand hill
by a dry well
but not afraid

the sun eats
in the still noon
from the seed's gland
but not afraid

the dogs whine
in the tan place
where the sun bleeds
on the tough earth
but not afraid

the sweat rains
in the matted place
in the month of blood
in the fur-bone cave
in the flat heat
in the moist spot
in the brown land
but not afraid

the drum breaks
in the spine
in the brain
in the nipples
in the knee caps
in the middle of tears
in the simple dream
of the red heart
but not afraid
but not afraid

Mama's Got The Blues

house lit up
me in party dress
in no party mood
I move in angles
blowing pink horns
I think
I hear ambulances
in the night
I tell you
they scare me
my daughter is ten
only child
of many cousins
she shines today
radiant as water
a song falls on her
sings itself
apart
upstairs
still
as an elevator shaft
my mother's life
thunders
and I am a heavy
wedge
of it
how does it feel
wedged in
the middle
white blue
and cracked
I mutter
obscenities
of wedgewood
shit

the old man say
never say
shit
say if you do
child
just you wait
child
I gonna wash
your little mouth
with soap
strong white streamin'
soap
that what
my daddy say
when can I go home
obviously bored into
I wish to be
as sane
as salty as anyone
slow-eyed and apron-hipped
waiting every night
for my hide hide
here comes the hunter
to come home
from the downtown heat
so I can love him up
and he can burn me down
here me dream
and lonely talk like this
and you know it
Mama's got the blues

Tucson Boogie

Sun so hot
I think
I'm mostly dead
leave
small mounds
on the sands
for you to know
my residue
all spice
strong and mild
weak and wild
all the same package
you know that
brother
you so smart
and me
with such intelligence
we quite a bundle
hot rocks on the
sand waste
scorched frog
makin' it
with some pre-
historic lizard
yippee yi yo
this here be
the wild west
hold on brother
to your chaps
afore
I pull them down
and you know what

like I told you
I would do
dry bones
grind to powder
blow sky-high
in desert
sands too hot
for hell-
bread or water
old glint eyes
2 paces behind
ready to shoot
me full of liquid
silver
that's what we said
we liked
this sparce clean look
to bones and belly-
button
saguaro boojum and prickly pear
no way out of the old corral
some old fart
gabby hayes or god the sandman
limps off into the desert
holdin' his sides
almost dyin'
laughin'

Bridge Burning

1.
when i was very small
i believed
that if i had a wound and
you touched it
you would feel the pain
and become the bridge

mama poppah
baybee how
suckah how
howzah

horsie fire
bear toes

fire in rain box
air full dirt rip

blood stop die o
o no mother o

swans o great soft mother swans gliding these waters
bumping dumbly on icecakes my father's first wife
like a poppy is chanting bright-red and wafer thin
in the chiseled silver january dawn

hello hello
a small child
in leggins'
calls up through

the ice-air
up to the lady
the poppy
is chanting

i am going
to die in these
snows before
the thaw

2.

my daughter turns in her dreams
my window blinks at a brick wall
I listen...pretend

I'm the wife again
taking giving courses
gourmet dinners   every hair
in place   but still...

I'm the upcountry other woman
see my scruffy turf
my kelp my milkweed

pods my adolescent onions
my worshipping tubors
my fluff...

think
i might have known
what it is like
to be you

whether
you hung around street corners leering
whispered incantations touched the bark of trees
put tin soldiers in your girl friend's pants
took three umbrella twirls and hit the dirt

I want to know!
My belly is empty
And I want to know

take me
take me
is heard

I can't
I can't
is heard

the words rise
and meet
in the middle air

Woman At The Window

hey you splutterer
you creeper you clenched
violet you warrior
rose you mop

come on out and play
forget the spiders
watching from the house
they have their webs
to worry on

find yourself a river
you thin nervous thing
and don't go back
in your dark denying hole
heavy with chants
and clanging dreams

don't go back
and chew on your dishes
until they crack

find yourself a river
girl and whistle to it
chop up your crosses child
and build yourself a raft
chop up your crosses sister
and burn the wood to keep you warm

hang prisms at the window
and let go lady hey
don't count the colors
when you come   flying through

Easter

The first upbeating of lost birds of the new days
of spring in time turning over in the spring upbeating
meaning time time turned over and ticked off in time
coming in and running out in time wasted and wanting
time like a cough like the flight of a crow in the black
search across skies time in the first morning of my old
age in the first wing-tipped warning of birds in a
woman grown suddenly young in the whiteness of cages in
a woman grown suddenly old in the whiteness of age in
the sudden carrying power   of age   in the black pursuing
powder of old age in the banner of it in the fierce ribbon
of age in the new day of old age in the first weight and
ways of old age in the sudden burden of it the repeating
the carrying toward the earth the sudden lurch into the new
daze of light the swift leaning the new learning the way
the eyes suddenly turn the swiftness of flowers their
terror the beat of their light their quick disappearance
into dark the dark disappearing of light the last sight
of it the giving over the sudden and painful dive
into the blind and lurching light.

She Is The Man She Loves

in the strange land
where mutilants pulse
and beat the air
she remembers the bells
their dry song
bigger than dream
and more grotesque
she stumbles
the dirt groans
the old crone warbles
she crouches
a contracted animal
in heat
her weight drags
to deliver
in the thunder
the old crone
screams
helpless
a red bird
stumbles
out

Light Sign

rock   a cactus plant
bell   a bowl   maybe two bowls
wide arcs of sand   sky

red-black bird of pain
your call marks this western sky
I want to touch you

the repetition
of motion   your name   my name
day   a door   then night

I hear the love poem
crack   inside a breaking   one
cry turns into two

A Bird Or A Beast

a bird
 or a beast
  or a reconstructed creature
  half-bird half-beast
    was born in that hurricane
     walked where the wrecked poplars
     swayed and spun into
      the eye of the storm

       song where song when
       bells all the morning long

Horses Move Across

horses move across unlighted landscapes
　of the dream. overhead the golden crows
　　form galaxies; in the foreground we are
　　　shown a room, a thousand corridors, some
　　　　place to move, falter, or become before
　　　　　the red storms come to scatter precious
　　　　　　emblems: horse crows men rooms all into
　　　　　　　a warmer place protected from the winds
　　　　　　　and sensed obscurities the mind can see

　　　　　　　and sensed obscurities the mind can see
　　　　　　　a warmer place protected from the winds
　　　　　　emblems: horse crows men rooms all into
　　　　　the red storms come to scatter precious
　　　　place to move, falter, or become before
　　　shown a room, a thousand corridors, some
　　form galaxies; in the foreground we are
　of the dream. overhead the golden crows
horses move across unlighted landscapes

Spell To Heal Wolf Bite

Ring Round in wolf-town. In
mean. In bite. In root. In safe-
town of mother-grown. In tear.
In father-rage. In ring round tear
in wolf-ground. In bright rip
in father-find. In bright father-
ground. In mother-bone. In mind.
In mother-rind. In moan in mother-bind.
bind. In wolf-rain. In father-bind.
In kind.In strong rain on wolf-
root. On tooth. On father-bound.
On tough wolf on rip. On ground.
On ripe bone. On wolf-sound on one.
On long wolf-howl on air. On long rip
on air. On ear. On land. On take. On
father-ground on hear. On hurt. On heal.
On sharp bite. On home. On heal. On out.
On done. On over. On out. On out, on Out.

Thirteenth Season Of The Old Crone

Out of the giant hole
                    into the gasp of air
                              the thrust and chant of morning

Into the loss of stars
                    the canopy of splinters
In time with the bear
                    with the muskrat
                              the staggering plants

The Old Crone crawls out from under
                    with winter as an incidental
                    she has come through

With water surrounding her hands
                    in the light of the spring and its high-
                              pitched cries   she has come through

She has come through
                    into a meadow of ice where flowers break
                              and burn   she has come through

Where children move enchanted into the promise of monsoon
                    where beasts befriend her nuzzling and wet
                              she walks where she must
                                        this long condition of flight

where birds with beaks like stilettos
          aim their chevrons carefully
                    where she marks time with migrations

where every night she digs on her hands and knees
    disappears into throats and nets
        scratches for snow and goldfish
           peers into the silt of caves

She is moved by the motion of insects
    their cries   their matings
        praying mantises eating each other's limbs

She looks for the moth and its shifting powders
    the stillness of stones in the drone of heat

She listens to the voices of relatives
    folded between the listless sleep of fossils
        traces the patterns of their careers   their crimes

She turns with the moon and its silver scars